D1591920

RANDY'S CORNER

DAY BY DAY WITH...

STEPHEN HILLENBURG

BY
JOANNE MATTERN

Mitchell Lane

PUBLISHERS

P.O. Box 196
Hockessin, Delaware 19707
Visit us on the web: www.mitchelllane.com
Comments? Email us:
mitchelllane@mitchelllane.com

Mitchell Lane
PUBLISHERS

Printing   1   2   3   4   5   6   7   8   9

RANDY'S CORNER

DAY BY DAY WITH. . .

Beyoncé	Mia Hamm
Bindi Sue Irwin	Miley Cyrus
Chloë Moretz	Selena Gomez
Dwayne "The Rock" Johnson	Shaun White
Eli Manning	Stephen Hillenburg
Justin Bieber	Taylor Swift
LeBron James	Willow Smith

Library of Congress Cataloging-in-Publication Data
Mattern, Joanne, 1963–
Day by day with Stephen Hillenburg / by Joanne Mattern.
   p. cm. — (Randy's corner)
Includes bibliographical references and index.
ISBN 978-1-61228-325-8 (library bound)
1. SpongeBob SquarePants (Television program) 2. Hillenburg, Stephen. I. Title.
PN1992.77.S68M38 2013
791.45'72 — dc23
                                                                                    2012018446
eBook ISBN: 9781612283944

ABOUT THE AUTHOR: Joanne Mattern is the author of more than 100 nonfiction books for children. Along with biographies, she has written extensively about animals, nature, history, sports, and foreign cultures. She lives near New York City with her husband and four children.

PUBLISHER'S NOTE: The following story has been thoroughly researched and to the best of our knowledge represents a true story. While every possible effort has been made to ensure accuracy, the publisher will not assume liability for damages caused by inaccuracies in the data and makes no warranty on the accuracy of the information contained herein. This story has not been authorized or endorsed by Stephen Hillenburg.

PLB

DAY BY DAY WITH **STEPHEN HILLENBURG**

Look! It's SpongeBob SquarePants! SpongeBob SquarePants is one of the world's most popular cartoon characters. He is loved by both kids and adults. SpongeBob was created by a man named Stephen Hillenburg.

Stephen McDannell Hillenburg was born on August 21, 1961, in Fort Sill, Oklahoma. When Stephen was little, his family moved to southern California. It was warm and sunny there, and Stephen loved to play on the beach.

Stephen also loved to watch cartoons. Bugs Bunny and Road Runner were two of his favorite cartoon characters. They had lots of funny adventures!

BUGS BUNNY

Stephen watched many films by Jacques Cousteau, who explored oceans all over the world. Jacques Cousteau made movies about the sea and the creatures that lived there.

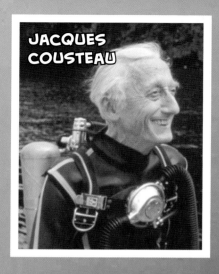

JACQUES COUSTEAU

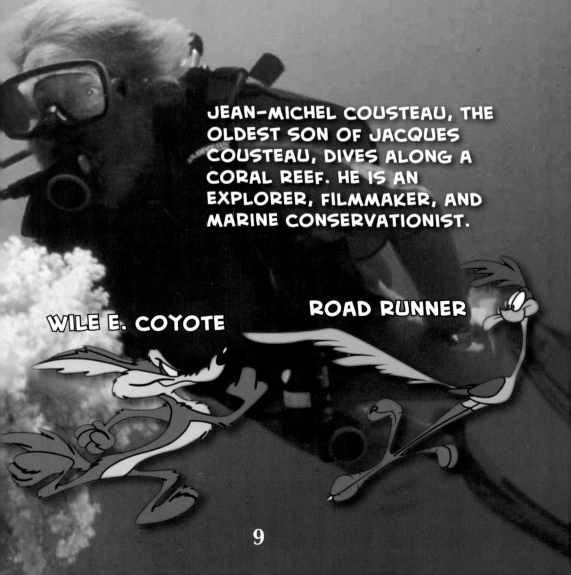

JEAN-MICHEL COUSTEAU, THE OLDEST SON OF JACQUES COUSTEAU, DIVES ALONG A CORAL REEF. HE IS AN EXPLORER, FILMMAKER, AND MARINE CONSERVATIONIST.

WILE E. COYOTE

ROAD RUNNER

When Stephen was 15, he went snorkeling. He loved swimming underwater with the fish, and he wanted to learn more about the world under the sea. After high school, he went to college and took lots of classes about the ocean and underwater animals.

Stephen got a job at the Ocean Institute in California, where people can go to learn about the ocean. But he found that he also loved to draw cartoons. He decided to go back to school to study animation, the art of making cartoons.

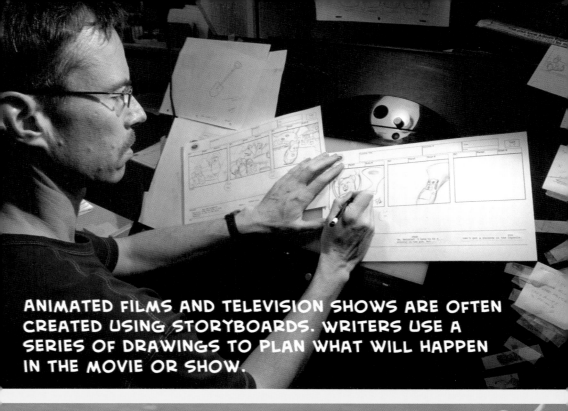

ANIMATED FILMS AND TELEVISION SHOWS ARE OFTEN CREATED USING STORYBOARDS. WRITERS USE A SERIES OF DRAWINGS TO PLAN WHAT WILL HAPPEN IN THE MOVIE OR SHOW.

Stephen went to art school, and after he graduated, he got a job at Nickelodeon. Stephen wrote stories and drew pictures for a cartoon called *Rocko's Modern Life*.

Stephen had fun working at Nickelodeon. He met many friends there. One friend was Tom Kenny, who would later become the voice of SpongeBob SquarePants.

TOM KENNY

16

Stephen decided to make his own TV cartoon about sea creatures. He wanted the main character to be a sea sponge. Stephen started drawing, and he drew a square, yellow sponge that looked like a kitchen sponge. He named the character SpongeBob SquarePants.

SANDY CHEEKS

PATRICK

PLANKTON

GARY

SPONGEBOB
SQUAREPANTS

18

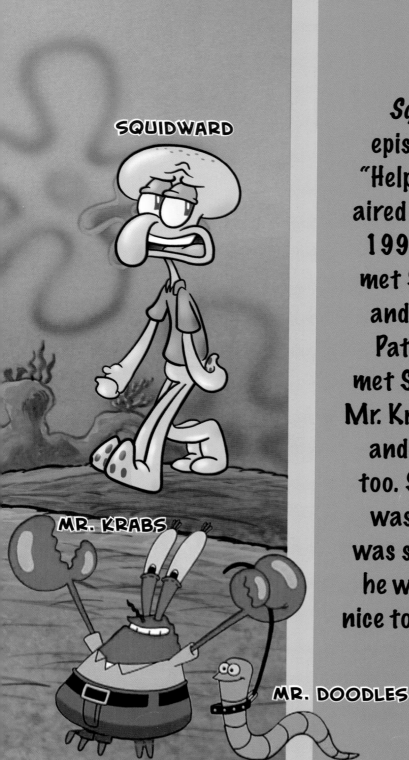

SQUIDWARD

MR. KRABS

MR. DOODLES

The first *SpongeBob SquarePants* episode, called "Help Wanted," aired on May 1, 1999. Viewers met SpongeBob and his friend Patrick. They met Squidward, Mr. Krabs, Gary, and Plankton, too. SpongeBob was funny, he was sweet, and he was always nice to everyone he met.

Everyone liked SpongeBob, and Stephen made more cartoons. When he and his friends talked, they would talk about things that happened to them when they were kids.

They talked about their moms and dads. Stephen and his friends used all those things to write funny stories for SpongeBob.

JELLYFISH FIELDS
MANY JELLYFISH LIVE HERE, AND THIS IS WHERE SPONGEBOB AND PATRICK GO JELLYFISHING. JELLYFISH CAVES CAN BE FOUND IN THE MIDDLE OF JELLYFISH FIELDS.

21

Making a cartoon takes a long time. Stephen draws pictures of SpongeBob and his friends. Then, other people make those pictures into moving cartoons. Finally, Tom Kenny and other actors add their voices. The SpongeBob cartoons are not made on a computer. They are all drawn by hand.

CARTOONIST HY EISMAN DRAWS A POPEYE CARTOON IN HIS HOME STUDIO. EISMAN KNEW BY THE AGE OF 5 THAT HE WANTED TO DRAW COMICS. HE WENT TO ART SCHOOL IN NEW YORK CITY, AND STARTED OUT WORKING FOR OTHER CARTOONISTS. HE TOOK OVER AS THE ARTIST FOR THE POPEYE CARTOONS IN 1994.

In 2004, Stephen and his friends made *The SpongeBob SquarePants Movie.*

Stephen directed the movie, helped write the story, and drew the pictures. He was in charge of everything that happened in the movie. The movie was a big hit and SpongeBob was even more popular!

BIGGER. BETTER. MORE ABSORBENT.

THE CAST MEMBERS OF *THE SPONGEBOB SQUAREPANTS MOVIE* FROM LEFT TO RIGHT: BILL FAGERBAKKE (VOICE OF PATRICK), DAVID HASSELHOFF (HIMSELF), SCARLETT JOHANSSON (VOICE OF MINDY), AND TOM KENNY (VOICE OF SPONGEBOB)

SpongeBob SquarePants is one of Nickelodeon's most popular shows. The cartoon has won many awards. Stephen and his friends enjoy meeting their fans and signing autographs.

ACTOR TOM KENNY (VOICE OF SPONGEBOB SQUAREPANTS) SIGNS AUTOGRAPHS AT THE HOLLYWOOD RADIO AND TELEVISION 10TH ANNUAL KIDS DAY, HELD ON AUGUST 18, 2004, IN HOLLYWOOD, CALIFORNIA.

THE CLASH OF TRITON

28

SpongeBob SquarePants is everywhere! He is on TV. There are SpongeBob games and books. There are SpongeBob clothes and dolls. Stephen makes sure everything runs well in SpongeBob's world.

STEPHEN AND HIS
WIFE KAREN
ATTEND THE
UPTON SINCLAIR
FUNDRAISING
BENEFIT

Stephen has fun living near the ocean with his wife and son. Stephen still loves to go to the beach, and he even loves to surf. Most of all, he loves thinking about the next adventure for his underwater buddy, SpongeBob SquarePants!

FURTHER READING

BOOKS

MacQuitty, Miranda. *Ocean*. New York: DK Children, 2008.

Yaccarino, Dan. *The Fantastic Undersea Life of Jacques Cousteau*. New York: Random House, 2012.

WORKS CONSULTED

Cavna, Michael. "The Interview: 'SpongeBob' Creator Stephen Hillenburg." *Washington Post*, July 14, 2009. http://voices. washingtonpost.com/comic-riffs/2009/07/_tom_kenny_who_voices.html

Levy, David. "Interview: Stephen Hillenburg." Animondays, February 11, 2012. http://animondays.blogspot. com/2012/02/animondays-interview-stephen-hillenburg.html

Metacritic. "Stephen Hillenburg." http://www.metacritic.com/person/stephen-hillenburg?filter-options=movies

"Nickelodeon's 'SpongeBob SquarePants' Reaches A Milestone: 10 Years." Access Hollywood, July 13, 2009.

WORKS CONSULTED

Stanley, Alessandra. "A Fun-Loving Sponge Who Keeps Things Clean." *The New York Times*, July 9, 2009.

How Stuff Works Express. "Under the Sea and On Top of the World: Stephen Hillenburg." http://express.howstuffworks.com/ep-shillenburg.htm

ON THE INTERNET

Nickelodeon: SpongeBob SquarePants http://spongebob.nick.com

SpongeBob SquarePants http://www.tv.com/shows/spongebob-squarepants

Stephen Hillenburg: IMDb http://www.imdb.com/name/nm0384864/

The Beginning of SpongeBob/ El Origen de Bob Esponja http://www.youtube.com/watch?v=6B3xMEzCXQs

INDEX